SOLDIERS IN UNIFORM

Du
During the Twentieth Century more men served with the British Army than at any time in history. In the nineteenth century, wars had been fought by professional soldiers in far away places. But the new century saw large numbers of volunteer soldiers supporting regular troops overseas for the first time. Subsequent events - two world wars, policing an empire and compulsory national service - means that many family photograph albums contain pictures of soldiers in uniform.

The uniforms, such as those above, may mean little to the current generation, but an understanding of what you should look for can reveal much about regiment, time and place. Whilst the left-hand photo shows only enough to indicate that the soldier is a private of The Royal Artillery around 1906, that on the right contains enough detail to identify the subject as an off-duty Second Lieutenant of The 1st Battalion, The South Wales Borderers, photographed between December 1942 and August 1944.

This guide describes the uniforms worn between 1900 and 1961 and explains what to look for in your pictures so that you can spot the relevant detail and thereby identify and date them. But Army uniforms are a complex subject and sadly a book this size cannot contain all the answers. In addition to the dozens of types of uniform shown in these pages, several thousand badges denoting regiment or corps, rank, trade or fighting formation were applied to Army uniforms during the last 100 years. Many much larger books would be needed to enable you to identify every aspect of the subject. This one concentrates on the first 60 years of the Twentieth Century where the experience of the world wars, policing the Empire and National Service were shared by most families. It provides an outline introduction to the styles of uniform worn by the British Army most likely to be found in family albums - where the majority of these pictures originated.

It must be stressed that the dates given are only a guide. Whilst uniforms were authorised from a certain date, they may not have been immediately adopted. The War Office issued constant reminders not to waste public money, ordering units to wear out old uniforms before taking new items into use. The introduction of Battle Dress, described later, provides a good example. Announced in March 1939, many units did not receive it until early 1940, whilst the superceded Service Dress jacket was retained and worn by many soldiers as a best uniform long after it was officially obsolete. It must also be pointed out that the British Army is a complex organisation. In the last century it has included amongst its officers and soldiers, Regulars and Territorials, volunteers and conscripts, specialists and tradesmen, men and women, whose dress might vary according to whether the wearer is a member of a Regiment or a Corps, a Regular or Territorial, an Officer or an Other Rank. If you are not familiar with the Army's organisation, you may find the section "Some Terms Explained" at the end of the book helpful.

BEFORE THE GREAT WAR - 1900 TO 1914

The years to 1914 saw the passing of the red coat, often seen as the mark of the British soldier in the nineteenth century. In fact, red coats were largely confined to the infantry - except for Rifle Regiments who wore dark green - whilst most cavalry and supporting arms wore blue. At home, the same style of uniform was worn for all duties. Full dress, reserved for major parades, was a best tunic worn with a distinctive regimental headdress. For most regiments this was a blue cloth helmet, the design copied from the German army, with fittings in brass or gilt for Regular soldiers, silver or white for Volunteers. Infantry regiments wore a spike atop the helmet, whilst supporting arms, especially those who rode horses, replaced this with a ball. A plate at the front of the helmet - the design varying according to regiment - carried the regimental badge at its centre. Introduced in 1878 and in general use from 1881 it is worn here by an Officer of the Royal Artillery (left) and a Private of The East Surrey Regiment. Fusiliers wore fur caps, Scottish regiments, feather bonnets or shakos – small peaked caps.

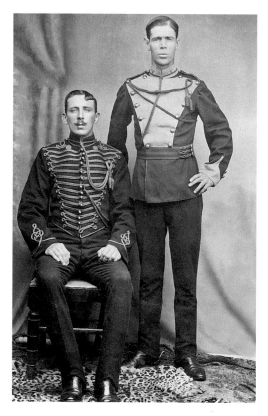

Tunics had coloured collars and cuffs which were known to the army as facings. Regiments with Royal in their title wore blue facings, Scottish regiments yellow, Irish regiments green and the majority of other regiments, white. The Corps and some cavalry regiments wore blue tunics but for historical reasons, cavalry regiments styled as Hussar or Lancers wore the distinctive styles shown in the photograph - a Lancer (right) and a Hussar (left). Badges of rank were worn on the shoulders by officers and on the arm by soldiers. Other regimental distinctions included badges on the collar, regimental buttons and the title of the regiment on the shoulder strap, either woven or in metal. A modified full dress, known as the undress uniform was worn by ORs for everyday duties with a second-best jacket and a cap replacing

the helmet. Until 1903 these included a round pillbox cap (left) for cavalry and artillery and a blue, Scottish-type, Glengarry cap with ribbon tails for the infantry. Following the short-lived Brodrick cap worn from 1903 to 1905 (see page seven), soldiers wore a peaked forage cap in regimental colours. When off duty outside barracks, they wore walking-out dress: undress uniform with a belt and a regimental "swagger cane" carried under the arm. The picture on page one illustrates this clearly.

For active service abroad – which usually meant an outpost of Empire - foreign service dress was worn. Made in khaki drill (KD) this lightweight uniform was introduced in India in the 1840s but by the end of the nineteenth century its use had spread to most of the British Army overseas. Widely adopted by troops fighting the Boer War in South Africa at the turn of the century, it is shown here worn with the off-duty Glengarry cap by a regimental signaller. The bandolier across the shoulders carried rifle ammunition and became very popular during the Boer War, replacing for many mounted troops the cumbersome leather personal equipment used in time of war. Queen Victoria thought khaki a hideous colour for her soldiers "and hoped that she may never see it in England". It took only a year from her death for her wishes to be ignored. The army learnt many valuable lessons about equipment, tactics and reserves from the Boer War, many of which were incorporated in the dress, equipment and organisation of the new century. One was the impracticality of the same uniform for both war and Home Service Dress (SD) was introduced in January 1902, replacing undress as the Army's uniform for everyday wear until 1939.

At first, SD for both officers (left, front) and other ranks (ORs) (right) had a closed collar, but in 1912 a new, open-neck pattern worn with collar and tie was introduced for officers. The differences are shown clearly in the photo below taken during the changeover period. Bronze badges on the collar, often worn in facing pairs, identified an officer's regiment. This pattern of jacket is still worn today, although many regiments introduced gilt or silver collar badges in the inter-war years, particularly after officers no longer wore SD for active service. No change was made to the pattern of jacket worn by other ranks.

As well as wearing a different jacket, officers were distinguished from other ranks by rank badges on the jacket cuff. These consisted of a series of light-coloured lace loops - the more senior the officer, the more loops – with a panel containing cloth versions of the stars and crowns worn on the full dress shoulder strap. Badges for a Second Lieutenant are shown below and those for a Lieutenant and Major in the photo to the left. Other Ranks, from Lance Corporal to Sergeant, wore from one to three cloth chevrons or stripes on each arm. In some units particularly cavalry, artillery and engineers, regimental badges were worn by Sergeants on or above these stripes.

Ranks above Sergeant wore badges of various designs above the stripes or in the case of Warrant Officers – the most senior of other ranks - on the wrist. Examples are shown on the next page.

ARM BADGES WORN BY OTHER RANKS

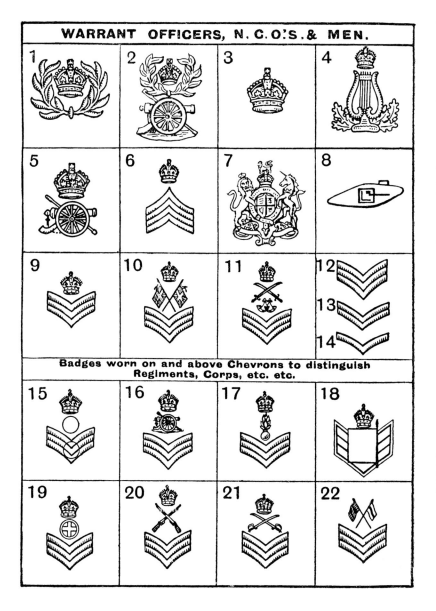

WARRANT OFFICERS, N.C.O.'S.& MEN.

Badges worn on and above Chevrons to distinguish Regiments, Corps, etc. etc.

WARRANT OFFICERS
1) First Class Staff Sgt Major
2) Master Gunner
3) Company Sgt Major
4) Bandmaster
5) Master Gunner 3rd Class
6) Squadron Cpl Major, Household Cavalry
7) Regimental Sgt Major

NCOs
8) Tank Corps Arm Badge (all ranks from 1917)
9) Quartermaster Sgt
10) Colour Sgt
11) Colour Sgt, Rifle Regiment
12) Sgt
13) Corporal
14) Lance-Corporal
15) Cavalry Regt Sgt with regimental arm badges
16) Artillery Sgt
17) Engineer Sgt
18) Foot Guards Sgt
19) Medical Corps Sgt
20) Musketry Staff
21) Gymnastic Staff
22) Assistant Instructor, Signalling

Shoulder straps on both patterns of officers' SD jackets were fixed, but the army took time to decide what to give ORs. From 1902 until 1904 straps were detachable, with a coloured edging and central stripe distinguishing the arm of service. A twisted shoulder cord was then used until 1907, when a fixed strap of the same material as the jacket was chosen.

At first, the soldier's regiment or corps was indicated on his jacket by a cloth shoulder title in standardised colours (below, left). Infantry regiments wore white letters on red with individual battalions identified by a separate number below the main title (below, centre). With the introduction of the fixed strap, cloth titles were replaced by metal shoulder titles (below, right) similar to those worn in India since the 1880s. Officers did not wear regimental titles on SD as their collar badges identified the regiment.

Dress for Highland Scottish regiments was the kilt with Highland shoes and khaki spats rather than boots and puttees, whilst Lowland regiments wore trews. Both were worn with a distinctive Scottish-style of SD jacket, the front bottom corners of which were cut-away to show off the sporran. Officers and ORs wore this jacket in different materials. Whilst ORs wore the same rank badges as English regiments, the rank lace on the officer's cuff in Scottish regiments was different. As can be seen on the right hand figure below, the lace ran around the top of the cuff with the rank badges sewn horizontally rather then vertically. Headdress for all ranks was the "fore-and-aft" glengarry cap with its distinctive ribbon tails. In some Scottish regiments a diced band was worn around the cap.

Whilst officers adopted a khaki version of the forage cap, it took some years before the army was happy with ORs headdress. Scottish regiments adopted the Glengarry as shown on the previous page, but English regiments experimented with several alternatives before arriving at an acceptable style. The first, adopted in January 1902, was a soft felt slouch hat (above, left) based on that worn in South Africa. Worn until 1903 this was replaced by the universally-detested, peak-less Brodrick cap (above, centre), named after the Secretary of State for War, but said to have been chosen personally by King Edward VII. Made in dark blue with regimental facings this was unsuitable for wear with field dress and a khaki cloth cover with a peak (above, right) was provided for the Brodrick in 1904.

In 1905 the army finally settled on the same style of headwear for ORs as for officers - a khaki version of the undress peaked forage cap to be known as the Service Dress (SD) cap (left). In the centre of the cap all ranks wore a cap badge, its design unique to each Regiment or Corps of the army - in this case that of the Royal Engineers. Badges were made in bronze for officers whilst ORs wore badges in brass, white metal, brass and white metal or, for rifle regiments, blackened brass, according to regimental tradition. The cap badge is the basic identifying feature of British army uniforms, clearly indicating regiment or corps. It often includes a crown or royal cypher, the pattern changing with the monarch - although it is common to see obsolete patterns of badge still being worn long after they should have been replaced. In 1914, some 150 different cap badges were worn by the British Army in the SD cap alone.

Service dress was completed by trousers, black boots (brown for officers) and some form of leg protection. From 1902 until 1907 short, black leather leggings previously worn on manoeuvres were in use. These were replaced by cloth puttees, which had been worn for some years on active service overseas and which were wound, bandage-like, from ankle to knee (far left), fastening with cloth tapes. Mounted units wore breeches instead of trousers, spurs on the boots and often wound their puttees from knee to ankle (left). Officers and mounted units wore various patterns of high legged boots and leather gaiters throughout the life of SD, particularly during the First World War.

After trials and tribulations, the dress of both officers (above, left) and ORs (above, right) had by 1914 settled into a style that was to remain basically unchanged for the next twenty-five years. But the Great War, as the First World War was known to its participants, with an unprecedented expansion of the British army and battlefield conditions that no-one could have predicted, saw numerous additions and modifications to the uniform of the British soldier.

THE GREAT WAR – 1914 to 1918

At the outbreak of the War in August 1914, Britain had a regular army of 163,000 men, backed up by volunteers and reservists numbering 268,000. In four years this grew to an army of 3,750,000 men, mainly engaged on the Western Front in France and Belgium, but also on active service in Italy, the Middle East and Africa.

No immediate changes were made to the army's uniform, although the hectic fighting in Europe in the summer of 1914 soon reduced the SD of all ranks to a dishevelled state. When on active service, a soldier added to his uniform a set of personal load-carrying equipment designed to hold ammunition, personal necessities and food to sustain him in battle. On the outbreak of the war this was the Webbing Equipment 1908 Pattern (left) approved after the Boer War. Consisting of a wide, woven cloth belt with brass fittings, at the front were two sets of rifle ammunition pouches, with a water bottle, bayonet and haversack carried on the sides and a pack on the back. Attached to the rear of the belt was a case for collapsible entrenching tool, the handle for which was secured to the bayonet scabbard. In the front line this was frequently supplemented with extra ammunition and trench stores, ranging from grenades to picks, shovels and barbed wire stakes.

As volunteers flocked to join the "Kitchener Battalions", equipment and clothing were in short supply. Two styles of emergency uniforms in blue cloth, known as "Kitchener Blue" (above centre and right) solved the problem of clothing until industry caught up in 1915. An emergency set of leather equipment, 1914 Pattern (above, left) was issued to the New Armies raised from these battalions which is easily identifiable by its box pouches and S-shaped buckle. Obsolete for most first line units by 1916, it remained in use for training battalions and some specialist troops, the belt being particularly popular for walking out.

Officers' equipment, which they bought at their own expense, posed different problems. The leather Sam Browne belt (named for the one-armed Indian Army officer who invented it), was worn with SD in peace and supplemented by a haversack and revolver holster for war. The belt (below left) quickly proved unsuitable for active service, becoming stiff and unmanageable in wet or cold. In addition it made officers easily identifiable, particularly in the early days of the war when they continued to carry swords into battle. By the winter of 1914 some front line officers were wearing the same webbing equipment as their soldiers (below, right) or buying an officer's pattern webbing from a private manufacturer.

Officers were also highly visible because of the rank badges on their cuffs, making them easy targets. Many also carried walking sticks - at first sight a strange fashion - but a practical aid to movement in the mud that quickly prevailed on the battlefield. Although sticks remained, by early 1915 rank badges began to be moved from the cuff to the shoulder strap as in full dress, making officers less obvious. In 1917 this practice was made official, individuals being allowed to choose between shoulder or cuff rank badges. In 1920 cuff badges were abolished and rank badges worn only on the shoulder straps, a practice continued to this day. Officers of the Brigade of Guards always wore rank badges on their shoulders and never wore cuff rank badges.

Headgear quickly underwent changes. The pre-war cap for both officers and ORs was fitted with a stiffening wire. On active service this quickly became uncomfortable and made headdress easily recognisable. The wires were quickly removed and caps assumed a battered shape - a difference clearly visible for both officers (left) and ORs (right).

A short-lived unofficial hat made an appearance in 1915, attempting to combine practicality with warmth. The "Gorblimey" cap - identifiable by ear flaps tied over the crown and said to be named for the effect its appearance would have on a Sergeant-Major - made a brief appearance until 1917 when a new soft version of the SD cap was introduced for ORs. Easily distinguishable by its stitched peak, it was designed to be taken off, folded and put inside a uniform jacket or pack. It remained official headdress for active service and manoeuvres until 1933. No matter what the headgear, the cap badge remained at its centre, with more than 20 new badges being introduced during the war for units raised as Kitchener battalions or to meet new conditions found on the battlefield.

As the army on the Western Front settled in to trench warfare, soldiers began to adapt to the conditions in which they found themselves. In the first winter of the war, the issue greatcoat with its long skirts (far left) became a liability in the mud. Men acquired fur coats of various styles from local sources or as presents from concerned friends at home. In 1916 these were replaced by an issue wool-lined leather jerkin, but for as long as they could retain them, the fur jacket was the mark of the "old soldier" who had served since the first winter of the war. Rubber boots and trench waders were also adopted to assist survival in muddy conditions.

As the soldiers sank below ground into the mud of trench warfare, their heads became vulnerable to falling shell fragments. Protection was found in the steel helmet which began to be issued in early 1916. For many, a desire to display regimental badges remained and these were often fixed to the front of helmets,

a practice banned in late 1917 when it was found that holes drilled for the badge weakened the helmet.

In April 1915 a terrible new weapon, poison gas, was used on the battlefield. Protection measures developed from a cloth mask across the face to a cloth helmet worn over the head, to a full-face, rubberised gas mask (left). Early helmets were carried in small cloth haversacks, but the larger, "small box respirator" introduced in 1916 required a large canvas haversack which, out of the front line was carried slung over the shoulder (far left). If gas attack was imminent it was worn on the chest, ready to be put on instantly (below). It remained part of the British soldier's equipment until the mid-1940s.

As the army grew in size, its organisation became more complex. A basic fighting formation, the Division - a combination of all arms and services organised to fight in support of each other - had existed in peacetime - but mainly on paper and with little chance to work together. As thousands of men went into battle, it became imperative to distinguish the troops of one division from another. Simple geometric symbols identifying formations were painted on vehicles from early 1915 and, although never universal, this practice was extended to the uniforms of the men from mid-1915. The majority of these "Divisional signs" were simple geometric designs applied in cloth at the top of the sleeves of the jacket.

Some designs were more ornate and easily identified, such as those of the 34th (left) and 30th (right) Divisions, the latter badge being a representation of the crest of the Earl of Derby.

The situation was further complicated when individual battalions began to apply cloth markings (below, left) to uniform. Originally the only unit marking was the brass shoulder title worn since the introduction of SD, but with some regiments having thirty or forty battalions it became essential to be able to tell them apart. Although some badges were quite ornate, simple shapes like those shown for the 10th and 14th Battalions (Bns) of The Hampshire Regiment, were more common. Usually worn on the arm, some units applied them to the back of the jacket just below the collar.

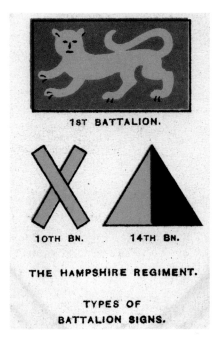

1ST BATTALION.

10TH BN.   14TH BN.

THE HAMPSHIRE REGIMENT.

TYPES OF
BATTALION SIGNS.

It was soon found that when worn with equipment and warm clothing, brass shoulder titles were not only difficult to see, but broke easily when loads were carried. Some units replaced metal titles with cloth ones similar to those worn from 1902 to 1905. Again worn at the top of the sleeve, these were more visible and could not be broken by rifles and equipment. As a result, from 1916, a dazzling array of cloth badges could be seen on the arms of British soldiers as cloth shoulder titles combined with formation and battalion signs.

As the war progressed, economy of scarce materials such as brass saw the introduction of an official cloth shoulder title, designed to slip over the shoulder strap and thus be easily removable prior to battle.Woven in white thread on a light khaki ground (below, left), these began to replace metal titles from 1916, although by February 1917 the authorities had realised that this form of unit marking would also be obscured by equipment and ordered slip-on titles to be sewn to the top of the shoulder, seen here (below, right) combined with a divisional sign on the arm and a unit cloth sign on the shoulder strap.

The greatest wartime changes were those that affected Scottish regiments. Highland shoes, worn with spats and diced hosetops (far left), gave way to boots socks and puttees, although the Highlanders steadfastly refused to abandon their kilts, which they covered with khaki aprons, a pocket at the front replacing the sporran. The easily-lost glengarry cap gave way to a highland bonnet (left), at first blue and later khaki. Known as a Tam O'Shanter (to the army a Cap, T.O.S.) this has remained the Scottish field headgear ever since although gradually reducing in size. At an early stage, the officer's TOS began to be made in a much lighter shade of material as it still is today.

With so large an army and the nature and scale of the fighting, numerous casualties were inevitable. Many a soldier wounded in battle on the Western Front in France and Belgium was brought home to England for treatment and convalescence in hospitals and nursing homes scattered throughout the country. Although in hospital, they were still considered to be serving with the army and were provided with a distinctive uniform which identified them as wounded soldiers. Known as Hospital Blues, these were cut on the lines of a two-piece suit. A single-breasted jacket of light blue cloth with a white lining was worn with blue trousers, a white shirt, red tie and the soldier's normal headdress. Rank badges were worn on the right arm only.

From 1916 Britain suffered manpower shortages and military service became compulsory. Fitness requirements were relaxed and some regiments recruited "Bantam" battalions from shorter men. With the Territorials serving overseas, invasion defence became the responsibility of a new force, the Volunteer Training Corps (VTC), recruited from older or unfit men. Originally raised locally, the VTC came under War Office control in late 1914. They were allowed a uniform, provided it was distinguishable from that of regular or territorial units. Two styles were made in grey-green cloth, one on the lines of a Norfolk jacket (far left), the other of normal army pattern (left), both worn with a red armlet on which was the royal cypher GR (Georgius Rex) in black letters.

Headdress was a peaked cap, although field service caps and slouch hats were also worn. Military badges were not allowed and VTC rank was indicated by braid on the cuffs (left). Renamed the Volunteer Force in April 1916 with units reorganised as local Volunteer Regiments, the grey-green uniform became official and the red armlet was abolished. In October of the same year, army rank badges were adopted and two months later khaki uniforms were introduced. In July 1918 Volunteer Regiments became volunteer battalions of line Regiments and adopted their badges with a V on the collar of officers. With the war over, Volunteer battalions were abolished in 1919.

A radical departure from tradition saw the arrival of women into the ranks of the British Army. Following an experiment in August 1915 with women cooks feeding the New Armies, the War Office was asked if it would consider employing women behind the lines in France. In early 1917 the Women's Army Auxiliary Corps (WAAC) was established with the first volunteers arriving in France in March.

Their chosen uniform was khaki in colour. Officers - known as Officials - wore a jacket with pockets in the skirt, fastened with a cloth belt (above, left). The skirts worn with it were full but for the time considered daringly short, being twelve inches off the ground. For the Other Ranks - known as Workers - the uniform was a practical, if unattractive, coatfrock in khaki gabardine with a brown washable collar (above, centre). A khaki greatcoat (above, right) was issued for cold weather.

All ranks wore a brown felt hat with a brim. Overseas, especially amongst drivers of motor vehicles, this was often replaced by a peaked cap with a storm-flap at the rear.

15

The WAAC's cap badge was the initial letters of the Corps within a laurel wreath, with the same initials in white on khaki worn on the shoulder straps of Other Ranks. Shoulder straps with coloured inserts indicated the type of work done - brown for clerks, red for domestic workers, claret for drivers and purple for women in other employments. An armlet lettered WAAC was sometimes worn on the greatcoat. In April 1918 the Corps was renamed Queen Mary's Army Auxiliary Corps and a new badge of the initials surmounted by a crown, replaced the old. Despite doing acknowledged valuable service, with over 57,000 women passing through the Corps, the QMAAC was disbanded in October 1919.

BETWEEN THE WARS – 1918 to 1939

After 1918, Service Dress became both working and ceremonial dress, with Full Dress abolished for the majority of the army, although available for state occasions and tattoos. An exception was made for The Household Brigade - the Household Cavalry and the five regiments of Foot Guards - who wore full dress for ceremonial from 1920. Although forced into Service Dress for everyday, the Foot Guards demanded a high standard of turnout, demonstrated here by recruits passing-out for service in 1922. Identifiable as Scots Guards by the chequered band on the coloured forage cap, they pose with instructors who are wearing the cap with the full dress tunic. The Household Brigade were the only regiments to wear the coloured forage cap regularly with SD between the wars. Until the late 1930s the Foot Guards retained the white leather equipment seen here (which had been abandoned by the rest of the army in 1908) for ceremonial duties.

As the army shrunk back to pre-war size – reduced to 207,000 men by 1927 - peacetime standards of dress reappeared. Caps regained their stiffeners, trousers were tailored more closely and puttees wound more tightly. An improved, more closely-fitted ORs "best" jacket introduced in 1924 meant that soldiers could wear regimental collar badges and buttons. The service chevrons on the Sergeant-Major's cuff - a reminder of wartime - disappeared in 1920.

Sergeants regained their sashes, and medals, primarily awarded for the conflict just ended, were seen again, worn here by the Sergeants of the 13th London (Kensington) Regiment, a Territorial Army (TA) unit, in 1924. Although officially abolished four years earlier, the seated officer still has cuff rank badges on his jacket, an example of personal economy measures.

The Regular Army spent these years acting as the policemen of Empire. After basic training at home, thousands of soldiers served in India or in the garrisons in Egypt, Malta, Sudan, Cyprus, Aden, Malaya, West Africa, Hong Kong and Singapore. Palestine, a British creation after the defeat of the Turks in the Great War, became an active service area from the mid-1930s as trouble flared between Jewish settlers and native Arabs.

In India, cheap labour meant no soldier did his own laundry and the standard of turnout was high, with highly-starched KD uniforms adorned with cloth and metal badges. These soldiers, identified by the cloth helmet badge as from the 2nd Bn, The Duke of Wellington's Regiment and newly arrived in India in 1929, typify the period. The one on the left is in duty dress - shorts and puttees over hosetops (woollen footless socks) in regimental colours. His companion, walking out in the evening, wears trousers to protect against the cold, a privately-purchased coloured field service cap and a swagger cane. Cloth badges on a regimental-coloured backing on the left arm indicate their trade and length of service.

Headdress for overseas service remained the distinctive Wolseley helmet, introduced in 1902. Made of cork and lined with silver foil, a cloth bandage known as a pagri or pugaree was wound around it to minimise the heat. Metal cap badges were replaced by coloured cloth flashes on the pagri, making for easy identification of regiments. Examples for the Somerset Light Infantry (left), Queen's Royal Regiment (centre) and Lancashire Fusiliers (right) are shown below.

In India the Wolseley was replaced from 1938 by the lighter khaki solar pith helmet (left) easily identifiable by its quilted finish, the two helmets often being worn side by side in the same unit (below, left). As with the Wolseley, coloured flashes were worn on the solar pith, here that of the Royal Artillery. Worn in the Middle East until 1942 when modern war made it obsolescent, the Wolseley continued to be official headdress in areas such as Jordan and the Sudan until finally abolished in 1948.

The soldiers above highlight a feature of operational uniform in India and other hot climates, where jackets were discarded and replaced by "shirt-sleeve order", with sleeves rolled up. The Other Rank's shirt of the period was made in grey wool, collarless and without pockets, so units often employed local tailors to make up better shirts or adapt the issue ones as a more comfortable and practical working dress. In the left-hand photo, pockets have been added to the issue shirt, whilst the sleeves have been shortened and the edges bound with tape, making a sensible and comfortable working uniform. Officers, who already possessed a shirt with collar, often added a pullover for cold weather duties in hot climates.

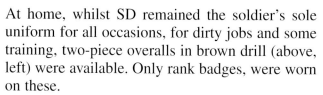

At home, whilst SD remained the soldier's sole uniform for all occasions, for dirty jobs and some training, two-piece overalls in brown drill (above, left) were available. Only rank badges, were worn on these.

In the mid-1930s the army sought to make its uniforms more comfortable to wear, easier to maintain and less conspicuous on the battlefield. In 1932 two infantry battalions - the Queen's Royal Regiment (above, right) and the Durham Light Infantry – carried out trials of an experimental uniform. Innovations included an open collar to the jacket, a shirt with attached collar and a soft hat with a cloth badge similar to that worn on the Wolseley helmet. Although popular with the soldiers – they were given shirts with collars and brass buttons and shoulder titles were eliminated - it was not adopted, although some features - notably the floppy hat - were to feature in the army's dress in later years.

Despite efforts by many regiments, Service Dress was still not deemed smart enough for what pre-war would have been full-dress occasions. Whilst planning the 1937 Coronation of King George VI, a new uniform was proposed. Worn and subsequently retained by all ranks who paraded on the day, Coronation Dress was to reappear after the Second World War. Modelled on an undress uniform known as Blue Patrols that originated in India, distinctive features included the use of the coloured forage cap for all ranks and trade and Warrant Officers' badges made in metal. Here a Sergeant of the Duke of Wellington's Regiment and the Coronation detachment of the 9th Battalion Royal Fusiliers – both TA units - parade in the uniform. Each has chosen a different style of belt.

Headdress between the wars was for most regiments the stiff SD cap, although its shape, for both officers (left) and men (centre) changed subtly - compare these two caps with those on pages four and seven. The difference between an officer's bronze cap badge and the brass one of an OR is noticeable. Inter-war headdress for manoeuvres or working was the soft SD cap with stitched peak, introduced in 1917, but stocks of this ran out in 1933 and it was replaced by the khaki field service (FS) cap (above, right). On the introduction of battle dress (see below), this became regulation headdress for the majority of the army, although never popular due to its tendency to fall off with the slightest exertion.

It is the Army's task to be sent wherever the government thinks fit. In some cases this requires additions to the standard uniform. In the late 1920s a civil war broke out in China and fears were expressed for the safety of British communities in the country. In 1930 the Queen's Royal Regiment found itself in Peking guarding the British legation against possible attack. The cold weather here resulted in an issue of fur caps, last used in operations against the Bolsheviks in Russia just after the First World War. Perhaps as a way of "flying the flag", even this unusual headdress prominently displays the regimental cap badge.

From March 1939, SD began to be replaced by Battle Dress (BD) (left). Said to be based on a ski-ing outfit and more suited to the demands of mechanised warfare, its introduction finally abolished brass buttons. Despite the 1932 trials of open-neck jackets and shirts with collars, BD again restricted ORs to a rough, closed-neck jacket with a collarless shirt and no tie. All ranks were to wear the FS cap with BD, although many officers, particularly in cavalry regiments, ignored this instruction and continued to wear their SD cap with BD.

Introduction of BD was slow, priority going to regular troops. TA units did not start to receive it until late 1939 and both regular and territorial units embarked for France in early 1940 still wearing SD. Despite protests, Scottish units adopted BD for active service mainly because no way could be found to make kilts proof against gas. Cumbersome long puttees were unsuitable for wear with BD and to

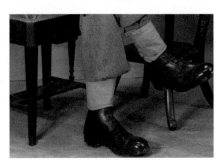

prevent the untidy and obviously unsoldierly look of the figure to the left, webbing anklets or gaiters fastening with leather or webbing straps, replaced them for wear with boots. A taller version of these had been on trial with the experimental uniform of 1932.

THE SECOND WORLD WAR 1939-1945

In September 1939 the British Expeditionary Force (BEF) set out for France, where, with Battle Dress not yet issued to all, both BD and SD were worn. The FS cap, replaced by the steel helmet when in action, was worn by most regiments, with the exception of Scottish and armoured units. The only insignia allowed on the BD jacket from 1939 to mid-1940 were cloth rank badges as worn on SD – on the arm for soldiers and on the shoulders for officers - and shoulder titles for ORs. Brass titles (below, left) were replaced by an easily removable cloth version embroidered in black on khaki (below, centre) but there are numerous instances of brass titles being worn with BD. Regimental pride - or lack of supplies - may explain this. Collar badges, not authorised for wear on BD were also regularly – and unofficially - seen (below, right).

Following its hasty departure from France in 1940, reconstruction of the army began in Britain. As a result of the operations in France it was agreed that lack of insignia on BD made it difficult to identify officers from soldiers and soldiers of different arms from one another when in battle. Practical measures to solve these problems included all officers wearing a shirt and tie with the collar of the BD open and placing officers' shoulder rank badges on a coloured cloth backing, different colours signifying the different arms of service. For ORs the identification of arms was solved by the introduction of an "arm of service" strip of coloured cloth (below, left) worn on both arms. At the same time, authority was given for units to wear distinctive cloth regimental markings on the arm (below, centre) and to paint similar markings on helmets (below, right). Helmet markings were to be identical to the cloth badges worn on the Wolseley helmet overseas and many cloth regimental arm badges were derived from the same source.

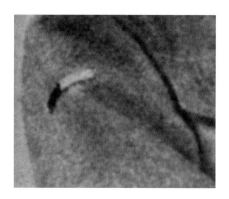  

Although initially banned, cloth divisional badges as worn in the First World War - now known as formation signs - made a comeback. Authorised in September 1940 only for fighting formations their use was quickly extended to most formations based in Britain, many of which would have had a fighting role if Britain had been invaded.

With a large part of the army in the UK training for operations overseas but deprived of action, the War Office felt that distinctive cloth insignia might help reinforce the identity and esprit de corps of units. After September 1940 therefore the arms of soldiers in the UK became a riot of colour displaying a formation sign, up to three arm-of-service strips and a cloth regimental badge. Typical examples shown below (left to right) are - The Royal Sussex Regiment, 44th Division with cut-out slip-on title, formation sign and three arm-of-service strips - Royal Engineers, 8th Armoured Division with brass title, formation sign and arm-of-service strip and 147th (Essex Yeomanry) Regiment, Royal Horse Artillery, 8th Armoured Brigade with formation sign, arm of service strip and regimental badge.

In 1943, after a long battle with several regiments who persisted in wearing unofficial regimental designations at the top of the sleeve – a distinction officially confined to the Household Brigade - the slip-on title was replaced for all regiments by a cloth arc at the top of the sleeve similar to, but smaller than, that introduced for SD in 1902. The 1902 colours were used for some of these shoulder titles, with infantry regiments again having their names in white letters on a red ground. Issue shoulder titles were printed but many units acquired embroidered examples at their own expense whilst individuals bought them from garrison tailors. A typical BD sleeve from July 1944 (left) shows the results. A trooper of the Royal Armoured Corps wears the Corps name in red on yellow, below which is the formation sign of 2nd Army and the RAC's yellow and red arm-of-service strip. Below the strip is the regimental badge of 107th Regiment Royal Armoured Corps, a converted infantry battalion of the King's Own Royal Regiment which has retained the design from its cap badge as its arm badge.

Battle Dress, both working and parade uniform throughout the war, altered its appearance in 1942 as a result of the need for economy of materials. Pleats and flaps disappeared from pockets and front buttons were left uncovered making austerity BD instantly recognisable. In September 1944 the army finally allowed ORs to wear shirts and ties off duty, although no issue of either was made for another five years. Soldiers either sacrificed the tail of their shirt or acquired an American army shirt.

The war resulted in a revolution in headdress that was to have a major effect on the army's future dress. In 1930 the Tank Corps, newly-formed during the First World War, had adopted a black beret, considering it more practical than the SD cap for working with tanks, being easier to keep on and not liable to show the oil stains inevitable in working with machines.

Originally unique to the Corps, (renamed the Royal Tank Regiment in 1940) (above, left), its use was extended in 1941 to all units of the Royal Armoured Corps (above, centre) which by that date included tank and cavalry regiments and even some infantry units (above, right) in a new role. Others found the beret a practical headdress and it was adopted in 1942 in maroon by the newly-formed airborne forces (far left) and in green by the Commandos.

In khaki (above right) it was authorised in 1942 for certain units including infantry battalions with armoured forces, staff officers and the Reconnaissance Corps but was widely worn by many others. If the FS cap was unpopular, its replacement the Cap, General Service (GS) (far left) introduced in September 1943 was deemed no better. Made like a khaki beret but of several pieces of cloth, many simply acquired a khaki beret in its place. From 1940 a version of the FS cap in regimental colours could be worn off duty, (above, right), which, although bought at the soldier's expense, brightened up the drabness of BD.

The standard steel helmet worn in action during this war (below, left) although superficially identical to that of the First World War was a slightly different shape with a more comfortable liner. Special pattern helmets were worn by specialists such as motorcyclists (below, centre) and airborne troops (below, right).

Whilst the larger part of the army trained in the UK for battle and an eventual return to Europe, the army overseas engaged the enemy - firstly Italians and then Germans - in Africa from 1940. Troops in the Middle East had from the late 1930s worn KD shirts with sleeves rolled up rather than the more constricting, closed-neck jacket, with trousers or shorts worn with long khaki socks. Headdress was the khaki Wolseley helmet (with a pagri flash) which the desert fighting of 1940 quickly proved unsuitable for modern war. Units ceased to wear it, replacing it in action with the steel helmet.

Out of the line soldiers wore their normal home service headgear, both caps FS and SD (below, left), with Highland units wearing the Cap, T.O.S. (below, right) and armoured units their black beret, a practical fashion copied by General Montgomery.

Although hot during the day, the African Desert was very cold after dark, making Battle Dress essential at night although, in the early days of desert warfare, not often available. Whilst ORs wore greatcoats, officers sported a splendid variety of non-issue garments, from cravats and pullovers to animal–skin coats. The Eighth Army, well known for its desert dress sense, even inspired a series of cartoons based on its eccentric fashions.

Troops in the Middle East at the start of the war were regular soldiers. As reinforcements began to arrive, UK dress distinctions came with them. Most obvious was the formation badge, apparent from mid-1941. As uniforms in hot climates needed regular washing, badges were designed to be easily removable, either by mounting them on cloth slides like those worn by officers for their rank badges (left) or by sewing press studs to the rear. Cloth shoulder titles and arm of service strips were rarely seen in the desert, although they became more widespread from 1943 as the desert armies were joined by units that had come directly from the UK to Tunisia. Once North Africa had been cleared of Germans, the troops moved via Sicily to Italy.

The Italian climate was closer to that of the United Kingdom. Whilst KD remained the uniform for hot weather, Battle Dress and greatcoats were required for winter. Because of the difficulties of supplying replacement clothing from Britain, many uniforms, particularly BD, were made by American companies and shipped directly to Italy. Known as War Aid (WA) garments, the BD jacket is easily identified by the large buttons on the breast pockets (left). Until the troops who had fought in Italy joined up in 1945 in Austria with those who had fought from Normandy, the WA blouse was an easy way to identify a soldier who had served in the Italian Campaign.

Although some Indian Army units fought in the Middle East, the majority of troops stationed in India and the Far East were, until the end of 1941, largely unaffected by the war. Uniforms and routines remained those of peace with highly-starched KD drill and a Wolseley helmet the standard dress. It seems not to have occurred to units stationed in Singapore and Burma that light-coloured khaki drill was not suited for operations in a jungle-green countryside. The arrival of the Imperial Japanese army in December 1941 challenged many of the army's existing practices.

Indian Army uniforms had long recognised the realities of the heat and dust of the continent and had evolved by the 1940s into a loose-fitting lightweight jacket with an open collar worn for work by all ranks.

Badges of rank for officers either in metal (far left) or in cloth (left) were worn on detachable straps. Where the rank badges were in cloth, the name of the regiment was often embroidered in black on the base of the strap, as here for a Lieutenant of the Royal Artillery (RA). The rank chevrons of ORs were represented by white tapes, usually only on the right arm.

Operations in Burma in early 1942 quickly proved that khaki was the wrong colour for jungles and the Indian clothing factories were soon hard at work turning out jungle green uniforms for British and Indian troops. The difference this change in uniforms made can be clearly seen in this contrast between the Engineer and Gunner officers.

Although a jungle green battle dress was produced, the four pocket "bush jacket" was usually preferred, with trousers replacing shorts as protection against the hazards of the jungle. For walking out, (left) the skirt of the jacket was tucked into the trousers like a shirt. Although destined to go through several changes of pattern and material the jungle green jacket and trousers were to remain the army's essential jungle fighting clothing for the next twenty years (see inside back cover). The floppy jungle hat was later widely worn in the jungles of Malaya.

As shown above, Caps SD or FS were worn when out of action but the tropical helmet, whether Wolseley or Indian pattern was of no use in the jungle and a more comfortable alternative to the steel helmet was sought as an operational headdress. The answer was the bush or slouch hat, a revival of the headdress worn in 1902 and used since then only in West Africa. Whether adopted on the arrival of West African troops in the Far East in mid-1943 or derived from a hat worn by Gurkha troops is not known but by 1943, the bush hat replaced any other form of operational headgear and was often worn for walking out. It was even authorised for troops returning to the UK. Apart from causing a permanent change in uniforms worn in tropical climates, the Japanese conquest of Malaya caused the army to look at its use of rubber and one item of equipment considered an essential in Europe - but rarely seen in the Desert or Far East - began to be used less frequently.

Since 1915, the respirator or gas mask had been carried on active service. Believing that the Germans had, and were ready to use poison gas, soldiers carried their gas mask at all times. On duty it was worn in the alert position on the chest, where it quickly became dirty from contact with the ground and the outline of items carried in it became very noticeable as can be seen in the photo to the left. A standard General Service respirator, developed from the small box respirator of the First World War, was carried until early 1944 when it started to be replaced by a smaller Light Assault mask, the case for which was carried slung over the shoulder. By 1945 even this was rarely worn.

The respirator case formed only part of the soldier's equipment. The introduction of a new weapon, the Bren light machine gun and the need for all infantrymen to carry its ammunition, saw the introduction of new webbing equipment. The 1937 pattern had a narrower belt than the 1908 pattern and the small, rifle ammunition pouches were replaced by two large box pouches (far left) for Bren gun magazines. Fastened to the pouches and carried on the back, a small pack contained essentials for the soldier in the field - dry socks, a towel, a mug and mess tins for food. Troops not armed with the Bren wore the belt - with smaller pouches designed to take rifle ammunition (above). The 1908 pattern equipment did not - disappear immediately. Used widely in France in 1939/40 it was frequently encountered in UK training units until mid-1941.

A new set of equipment arrived in the spring of 1940 when invasion of Britain was feared. With Territorials on active service and the army training to repel invaders, no force existed for local defence. In May 1940 the Local Defence Volunteers (LDV) were formed, being renamed the Home Guard (HG) in July, recruiting from men not required or able to undertake service with the army. Originally given an infantry role, they later undertook such tasks as manning the anti-aircraft defences of the UK. Dressed at first in denim overalls (left), with only a cloth armband to identify them, by 1942 the HG had acquired battle dress and a set of personal equipment suited to their role (above right). Dressed identically to regular troops, only the equipment, Home Guard shoulder titles and a two-piece cloth arm badge with the initials of the county in which they served and the number of the battalion within that county, identified them as Home Guardsmen.

Anticipating manpower shortages, the Army turned again to women to fill its ranks and replace men in support services, creating in 1938 the Auxiliary Territorial Service (ATS) to recruit women to serve as part-timers alongside the TA. Turned into a female army on the outbreak of war, it remained an all-volunteer force until December 1941 when women became liable for the call-up and service with the ATS. The uniform originally issued to the ATS (below, left) consisted of a khaki jacket similar in cut to the officer's service dress worn with collar and tie, skirt, stockings and brown shoes. Some Scottish units wore kilts instead of khaki skirts with the uniform jacket. The unflattering issue cap (left), similar to that of the First World War motor driver was replaced in 1941 by a slightly less severe version with a leather cap strap.

ATS insignia included a distinctive cap badge and a brass shoulder title for ORs. Officers wore a smaller bronze version of the cap badge on their collars. After a brief period of wearing badges of a unique ATS pattern, officers and NCOs wore army-style badges of rank. To reflect the importance of their work, many units authorised ATS serving with them to wear their cap or collar badge above the left breast pocket, as with the badges of the Royal Corps of Signals (left) and the Royal Artillery (below) Those ATS serving with formations who wore them also adopted formation signs.

Off duty, many ATS bought and wore the more flattering, field service cap in beech brown, piped with green, here (far left) worn by a Private wearing the distinctions of the Royal Artillery and serving in Anti-Aircraft Command, a major employer of ATS after 1941. The employment of girls on gun sites – where they did all the jobs except fire the guns - demanded a more practical uniform than skirt and jacket and in 1942 Battle Dress for women was introduced, worn with brown boots and anklets. Similar BD was worn in Europe by army nurses.

By 1945 over 190,000 women were serving with the ATS at home and abroad, supporting the work of 2.8 million soldiers in a far greater variety of jobs than had been envisaged before the war.

AN UNEASY PEACE 1946-1963

As in 1918, the numbers of men and women serving with the army shrank enormously when peace was declared, over half a million men and 31,000 women being released from service in January 1946 alone. But the Labour Government took the decision that conscription for National Service, introduced in 1939, should be retained and that young men, on reaching the age of 18 should be liable for military service. For the next 18 years more young men experienced the rigours of soldiering than had ever done so before in peacetime.

The army ended the war universally clad in BD which, in various patterns, remained its dress until the mid-1960s. It had proved so practical a uniform that it was adopted by the RAF and the Royal Navy – as well as the Germans and Americans. The collar and tie allowed off-duty in 1944 were allowed on duty from 1947 when a pattern of BD was introduced that was worn open, but could be closed at the neck. By 1949, the need for this vanished and the 1949 pattern blouse had a fully-tailored, stepped collar, recognisable by the single buttonhole on the left lapel. Ever wary of wasting money, the Army issued and allowed many varieties of BD – three different styles are visible in the left-hand photo above – in the immediate post-war years. It was the mid-1950s before the 1949 pattern (above, right) was used by all. Wearing the collar open required a proper shirt and, although as can be seen in the photos above, shirts and ties varied enormously in colour and shade, shirt-sleeve order became popular as training dress in hot weather.

A more dramatic change came with the gradual introduction of the beret as the universal headdress. The detested Cap, G.S. gave way between 1947 and 1949 to a khaki beret for most regiments (far left) except airborne forces and the Royal Tank Regiment who retained the maroon and black versions. In 1950 a blue beret was adopted as standard for all except Scottish, parachute and tank regiments, being worn at home and abroad for normal duties. A few units – mainly the Guards, Royal Horse Artillery and Military Police - retained the SD cap, often with a steeply raked peak (left).

Coronation Dress of 1937, suggested in July 1938 as a future parade dress for the army, was revived after the war in 1946 when HM The King, inspected a parade of men at Buckingham Palace in the army's new uniform, No 1 Dress. Colloquially known as "Blues" it was officially announced in May 1947 as the ceremonial dress for all ranks of both Regular and Territorial armies in peacetime, although it was some years before it arrived in quantity. From 1950, officers and senior NCOs were entitled to wear it on a variety of occasions both on and off duty, and it became standard dress for military bands. In 1951 it was sanctioned as a uniform for all other ranks. Worn with either the beret or peaked cap of regimental pattern, all badges on the jacket were embroidered in gold or silver wire on a coloured backing which for the majority of regiments was blue or red, but with many regimental variations. The original belt was a webbing girdle in regimental colours, fastening with a brass locket (above, left) but this was little used, being quickly replaced in most regiments by blue cloth belts or whitened 1937-pattern belts. No1 Dress provided a perfect background for the display of regimental dress distinctions. Collar badges were worn and cavalry regiments adopted chain mail on their shoulders, worn as a reminder of a once practical means of preventing sword cuts. Musicians wore regimentally-coloured cords draped across their chests.

Few National Servicemen were ever issued with "Blues" and undoubtedly, the dress recalled by most men serving with the army from 1945 is Battle Dress. In the more relaxed days of peace with time for "proper soldiering", regimental distinctions on this uniform mushroomed. The young sergeant to the left is typical of a 1950s soldier. His 1949 BD has cloth shoulder titles announcing him as serving with the Royal Corps of Signals, a formation sign to show he is serving at Catterick, a unit marking to distinguish him as a member of a training regiment and the distinctive metal arm badge of his Corps above his rank stripes, which are specially whitened. His 1937-pattern belt is blancoed and the brasses highly polished. Although not shown here, regiments could, from 1952, wear collar badges on BD whilst most cavalry regiments wore metal shoulder titles in preference to cloth ones.

The post-war period saw many developments in the British Army as the nature of war changed, the Cold War arrived and the British Empire shrunk. Special cold weather clothing – adopted in a modified form as combat dress in 1961– was worn in the Korean War of the early 1950s. Soldiers dressed in jungle green clothing saw action in Kenya and Malaya (see inside back cover) and in khaki drill in Suez, Cyprus and Aden. The Territorial Army shrunk in size as the need for conventional anti-aircraft defences in an age of missiles, disappeared. Women became a permanent part of the army, first as the post-war ATS and then from 1949 as the Women's Royal Army Corps, whose uniform remained BD with a green beret for many years (see back cover).

By 1961 the government had decided that, despite the perceived threat from the Warsaw Pact countries led by the Soviet Union, there was no need for peacetime conscription and that a future army would be recruited from volunteers. This reduction in size was taken as the opportunity to introduce a new uniform for parades and day-to-day duties. Based on officers Service Dress, No 2 Dress (far left) was introduced in 1961 as a Temperate Parade Uniform. Worn with a regimental headdress - usually the coloured peaked cap or beret - this remains the army's best uniform. Rank and trade badges worn on the uniform were reduced to two-thirds their previous size. It took some time to reach the army as a whole and the TA were still wearing BD whilst their regular counterparts were in No2 Dress (above, right). Many TA units did not receive No 2 Dress until after the major reforms of 1967 which saw the volunteer forces drastically pruned.

This short account of British Army uniforms ends with the arrival of No 2 Dress - still the main parade uniform of the army, although rarely worn. The dress and equipment of the last forty years covers such a wide range that it would require a further book and must remain outside the coverage of this one. Perhaps most importantly for the family historian, with the abolition of National Service, a smaller Regular Army and a Territorial Army that, compared with the 1950s, has almost vanished, fewer family members experience army life, so fewer families have photos of uniformed soldiers they wish to identify. Perhaps more importantly those shown in the photographs are still alive to explain them!

As explained at the outset, the intention of this book was to provide an introductory guide. Hopefully, readers can now take their first steps in establishing whether the ancestors shown in their family albums served in the First or Second World Wars, between or after these conflicts, and which identifying features to look for in the photos. Wardens Publishing provide a reasonably-priced identification service if you require further help.

For details please write enclosing a stamped self-addressed envelope to :

Wardens Publishing (IDs)
11 Malvern Road
Orpington
Kent
BR6 9HA

Or e-mail cdwardens@yahoo.co.uk for details

SOME TERMS EXPLAINED.......
The British Army distinguishes between troops who fight - the Cavalry (now armoured), Infantry, Artillery and Engineers - known as "The Arms" - and those who support them – "The Services". Uniform styles have reflected this distinction. The "building block" for Cavalry and Infantry is The Regiment. Whilst a Cavalry Regiment is a single unit with a distinct identity, Infantry Regiments (identified from 1881 with the counties of Britain) can have several Battalions (600-1000 men), each with their own customs and distinctions. In war the number of battalions in each infantry regiment may multiply - First World War regiments often had over 30. The Corps of Engineers and Artillery are large all-embracing bodies, separate units being identified by the type of role they perform. Here variations in dress and insignia are fewer. The Services support front line troops with cooks, policemen, drivers, mechanics, doctors and priests. These soldiers belong to a specific Corps – for example, The Army Catering Corps, Corps of Military Police or The Royal Army Ordnance Corps - each with a distinctive badge. Here again dress distinctions are fewer.

OFFICER OR OTHER RANK?... Different styles of uniform distinguish officers from their men. Commissioned by the Sovereign, Officers wear more ornate uniforms in better quality material, bought at their own expense, but tailored to regimental – and often their own - requirements. Other Ranks (ORs) – by definition anyone who is not an officer - are provided with their uniform by the army. Theoretically this is identical for all soldiers, although regiments introduced variations and individuals had uniforms tailored for a smarter appearance.

REGULAR OR VOLUNTEER?... Men enlisting into the army as their full-time job are known as Regular soldiers. But Britain has a tradition of volunteer reserve soldiers - civilians undertaking military training in their spare time in locally-based units. In the nineteenth Century, they served to defend Britain against invasion, but the Boer War saw volunteers overseas in support of overstretched Regulars for the first time. Known in 1900 as the Volunteer Force, these reserves were renamed the Territorial Force in 1908 and the Territorial Army in 1920, each change imposing a greater commitment to overseas service. At the beginning of the century volunteer soldiers could be identified by variations in dress, but these grew fewer as the century went on.

WARTIME SOLDIERS... In August 1914 huge numbers of men volunteered for Army service. Lord Kitchener, Minister for War, distrustful of the Territorials – he called them "a Town Clerk's Army"- created a new force from these volunteers. "Kitchener Battalions", often raised from cities or professions, were so numerous that at first they trained in civilian clothes or an emergency uniform, but by 1916 when first tested in battle, they had become an integral part of the army, often referred to as the "New Armies". Kitchener's prejudices were overcome by demands for manpower and Territorial Battalions took a full part in the war. On active service, differences between Regular, Territorial and Kitchener Battalions became blurred and all took reinforcements from wherever they could. Compulsory military service – conscription – was introduced in January 1916. During the Second World War, although some volunteering was allowed, recruiting was severely controlled. Whilst awaiting call-up, men of military age were placed on a national register to ensure that skilled workers were not lost from industry. Local connections of Territorial Army units were gradually diluted by wartime conscripts and no local units were formed, as the First World War had seen whole communities devastated by losses to local units in a single battle.

ORGANISED FOR FIGHTING... Regiments and Corps are grouped together as fighting formations in wartime. Battalions and Regiments combine into Brigades, Brigades into Divisions, Divisions into Corps, Corps into Armies and Army Groups, each with their supporting services. During the First World War troops in the same fighting formation wore a cloth badge on the uniform, to indicate their formation. These Divisional signs were abolished at the end of the First World War, although retained by some Territorial formations. Reintroduced as Formation signs in 1940, their use was widespread by 1943. They continued to be widely worn until BD was abolished.